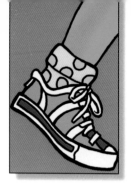

First Sports Science

In the
Gym

Nikki Bundey

 Carolrhoda Books, Inc. Minneapolis

All words that appear in **bold** are explained in Words We Use, which begins on page 30.

This edition first published in the United States in 1999 by Carolrhoda Books, Inc.

Photographs courtesy of:

cover (background), 4t, 6t, 13, 14b, 16t, 18t & b, 19, 20t, 22t & b, 23, 24t & b, 25, 26t & b, 27, 28b / Action Plus; Christopher Cormack - title page, 4b, 9t, 14t / Rupert Conant 5 / Peter Arkell 12t / Bruce Stephens 16b / Ray Roberts 17 / Caroline Penn 28t / Impact Photos; 12b / Sporting Pictures (U.K.); G Contorakes 6b / M Azavedo 7 / Bruce Fleming 8t / J Wender 8b / Viesti Associates 10 / Steve Ross 29 / TRIP.

Illustrations by Virginia Gray

A ZOË BOOK

Copyright © 1998 by Zoë Books Limited. First published in 1998 by Zoë Books Limited, Winchester, England.

Carolrhoda Books, Inc. c/o The Lerner Publishing Group
241 First Avenue North, Minneapolis, MN 55401 U.S.A.
Website address: www.lernerbooks.com

Library of Congress Cataloging-in-Publication Data

Bundey. Nikki.
    In the gym / Nikki Bundey: [illustrations by Virginia Gray].
        p. cm. — (First sports science)
    Includes index
    Summary: Presents some basic information about such concepts of physics as force and resistance, while describing the mechanics of gymnastics and other games and exercises that commonly take place in gyms.
    ISBN 1-57505-358-6 (alk. paper)
    1. Gymnastics—Juvenile literature. 2. Physical education and training—Juvenile literature. 3. Physics—Juvenile literature. [1. Gymnastics. 2. Exercise. 3. Force and energy.] I. Gray. Virginia. ill. II. Title. III. Series.
GV461.B88 1999
613.7'1—dc21   98-25064

Printed in Hong Kong
Bound in the United States of America

1 2 3 4 5 6 O/S 04 03 02 01 00 99

Contents

Indoor Fitness

The word gym is short for **gymnasium**, a Greek word for a building where people go to keep fit. Long ago, the ancient Greeks and Romans enjoyed physical exercise. Today, all kinds of exercise, music and movement, weight lifting, sports training, and games take place in gyms.

A handstand is hard to do even on the ground. This gymnast is doing a handstand on a narrow **balance beam**! She needs a very good sense of **balance**.

The younger you are when you start physical exercise, the better. Some **gymnasts** have become Olympic champions at the age of fourteen.

Many sports are played in gyms. Some are team games such as basketball and volleyball. There are also several types of gymnastics. **Artistic gymnasts** use bars, beams, mats, and **horses**. **Rhythmic gymnasts** move to music. Sports **acrobats** tumble and roll. All forms of gymnastics involve strength, **flexibility**, skill – and science!

People may go to a gym during their lunch break or on the way home. They exercise, or work out, with weights or other equipment that keeps them fit.

Exercise Science

What happens when we work out in the gym? Our lungs breathe in air, which contains a life-giving gas called **oxygen**. This gas passes into the blood and the heart pumps it around the body. Oxygen mixes with other substances in the muscles. This produces energy, the power to do things.

If the muscles do not get enough oxygen, they tighten up. When muscles are stiff, they begin to ache. Jumping rope can help to keep muscles loose and supple.

Keeping up exercise like this for half an hour or more uses a lot of oxygen. It is called **aerobic** exercise.

When we work out, we sweat, and our faces turn red. This helps to control our body temperature. The tiny **blood vessels** near the surface of the body open up so that we lose more heat through the skin. Sweating keeps us cool, too. The water in the sweat **evaporates** into the air around the body.

Sweating keeps the body cool during hard exercise. Sweat contains water, salts, and wastes from the body.

Safety in the Gym

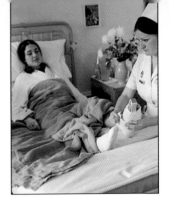

In a gym, the equipment is designed for safety. But even there, accidents can happen. Never use any equipment until you have been shown how. If there is an

An accident in the gym could result in a twisted ankle or even a broken leg. Make sure that the equipment you are using is correctly set up. Always use mats for exercise on the floor.

Never train alone. Always make sure that an instructor or other **spotter** is there to make sure you don't get hurt.

accident, get help from the instructor right away.

Be careful and prevent accidents:

- Do not push yourself too hard. If you don't feel well, stop and tell the instructor.

- Never exercise with anything in your mouth. Chewing gum might stick in your throat and choke you.

- Never exercise wearing jewelry. It might get caught on the **apparatus**.

- Never start your run-up to the apparatus before the person in front has cleared it.

Mats are made of rubber or plastic. These are **elastic** materials. When they are hit, they return to their original shape. If you fall to the ground, mats bounce back and cushion the **impact** of your fall.

Ready for Action

Fitness is a way of life — it doesn't start in the gym. You need regular rest and sleep. You also need to eat a balanced diet of healthy food. The vitamins in the food we eat keep us alert and in good health. Avoid too many fatty and sugary foods. Don't eat too much before exercise.

To stay healthy, you need to eat a variety of fresh foods. A natural chemical called Vitamin C occurs in many fresh fruits and vegetables. It helps the body to make use of other minerals, such as iron, that are found in food.

Before you start to work out in the gym, try some gentle warm-up exercises. You might touch your toes, bend sideways, crouch and stretch, or jump rope. The aim is to warm up, or loosen, your muscles so that they do not **cramp**. Do exercises like these after your workout, too.

Warm-up exercises help to get oxygen to the muscles. They have an aerobic effect. They also make you alert and ready to concentrate on the tasks ahead.

jumping rope   bending sideways   touching toes

Leotards and Chalk

Most people wear a T-shirt, shorts, and athletic shoes for gym sports. For gymnastic competitions, girls and women wear a leotard, while boys and men wear a jersey with pants or shorts. Footwear includes special lightweight slippers. Some gymnasts prefer to do the exercises with bare feet. The skin is sensitive and allows feeling while

Whatever you wear for gymnastics, make sure it doesn't get in the way of your movements.

This gymnast's leotard is close-fitting, which helps her move through the air easily. Gymnasts wear their hair short or tie it back.

giving a good grip. This gripping or rubbing force is called **friction**.

Gymnasts wear light, tight-fitting clothes. Loose, flapping clothes can catch on the apparatus or slow down the body through **wind resistance**. For smooth movement through the air, the body must be as **streamlined** as possible.

Gymnasts usually rub their hands with chalk. This provides extra friction for a good grip. Rough surfaces catch against each other with less slipping and sliding than smooth surfaces.

The Basics

Learning the skills of gymnastics takes time. Young children may start their work in the gym with simple movements to music. They may run indoor races, play tag in teams, or throw balls back and forth. Then they may try simple

Moving in time to music helps to give us a sense of rhythm. This is important for gymnastics and for many other sports.

These children are learning some moves used in ballet. Ballet and other dance moves are used in some types of gymnastics.

somersaults or handstands against the wall.

We use our brains for sports and gymnastics just as we do for math and reading. The brain is the control center of the body. It receives signals from other parts of the body, such as the eye or the hand, that record sight or touch. These signals travel along nerves. The brain sends back signals to muscles and **tendons** to move the limbs.

Balance is very important in gymnastics. Inside your ears are coiled tubes full of a liquid that moves as you move. Tiny hairs in the coils record the movement. They send signals to the brain to help you keep your balance.

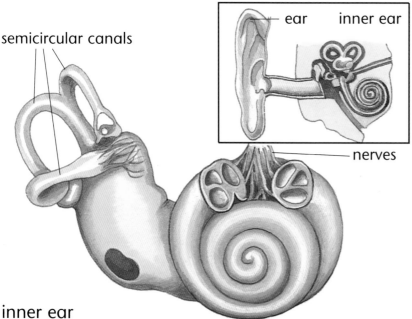

semicircular canals

ear   inner ear

nerves

inner ear

Training for Strength

People often use a gym to train for team sports. It is a good place to build up the strength of the arm and leg muscles. People make a **circuit** of the gym, using apparatuses such as exercise machines and weights. They may do stepping exercises on benches or climb ropes.

In some gyms there are special climbing walls. You climb them using both arms and legs. The force of **gravity** pulls your body down towards the ground. You have to pull and push against it.

Runners may want to build up their leg muscles, while throwers need to have strong arm muscles. Football players may use the gym to build their strength, or stamina.

The more you use your body, the better it works. A strong heart is able to pump more blood to the fibers of your muscles. The blood carries the extra oxygen that the fibers need to stretch and contract. It is this muscle movement that gives the body strength.

Special weight machines can be used to build up your muscle power.

18

On the Floor

Artistic gymnastics includes many different floor exercises. Performers can do handstands and **cartwheels**, **splits**, **handsprings**, and **roundoffs**. There are forward and backward rolls and somersaults. Gymnasts have to perform with the grace of ballet dancers.

As the judges watch this Russian Olympic gymnast, they check each movement she makes. They also judge how the movements are linked together.

To perform splits like these, a gymnast must be very flexible.

Different forces affect the body as it moves. Gravity pulls it downward. The movements of the muscles give the body upward, forward, or backward **thrust**. The force that keeps the body moving is called **impetus**. The friction of the body and the mat can slow down movement or bring it to a stop.

Each movement and landing on the mat should be finished without stumbling.

Vaulting

A vault is a leap over an object. When we play leapfrog, we are doing a type of vault. In gymnastics there are many different styles of vaulting. Some of these are combined with other gymnastic skills, such as twists or handsprings.

This gymnast's whole body twists around as he vaults over the horse.

A vaulting horse is a raised block. The block is stuffed and covered in leather. Girls vault over it sideways, and boys lengthwise.

Vaults usually begin with a running start. This increases the impetus needed to carry the body forward over the horse. For some vaults, gymnasts take off from a wooden springboard. Its bounce helps give upward thrust for the jump. You will land with greater force, so the mat is thicker than the one used in the floor exercise.

Bars and Beams

In the gym, bars are used for swings, turns, circles, and handstands. Gravity pulls at the body as it hangs from the bar. It takes strength to work against this force.

All bar work builds up strong muscles in the shoulders, arms, and stomach.

Uneven parallel bars have one bar higher than the other. **Parallel bars** are used in boys' and men's gymnastics. So is the **horizontal bar** or high bar.

Different forces affect the body as it whirls around the bar. It tries to fly outward, but is held back by the hand gripping the bar.

The point at which an object balances is called its center of gravity. When you move on the beam, your center of gravity changes and you may wobble. Stretching out an arm or a leg may help you balance again.

The balance beam is a single bar which is covered in soft suede. It is usually 16 feet long and 4 inches wide, and it is set almost 4 feet off the ground. On this narrow strip, the gymnast must learn to walk, run, jump, leap, do handstands and flips, and turn. These skills require a very good sense of balance.

Rings and Pommels

The rings offer some of the toughest exercises of all for male gymnasts. The rings hang from steel wires more than 8 feet above the floor. The gymnast grips the rings in his hands and then raises his body into swinging positions and even handstands.

Ring exercises put great strain on the arm muscles. For beginners, this strain can be eased if a spotter supports the legs.

The gymnast uses the rings as a type of **lever**. When the gymnast pushes against the rings, his body is forced to move.

Some vaulting horses have curved handles called **pommels** on the top. Gymnasts grip these in their hands as they vault and circle, swinging their legs. In competitions, they cannot touch the horse except with their hands.

Gymnasts need very strong arm and shoulder muscles. They swing around using the pommels of a pommel horse as a lever.

Grace and Agility

Rhythmic gymnastics is a mixture of dance and physical exercises such as turns, rolls, and jumps. Girls have to move gracefully in time to the music. They may use ropes for skipping, stepping, and throwing, or ribbons to swirl through the air. They may pass hoops over the body or throw and catch balls or clubs.

The ribbon floats through the air in spirals and loops. It matches the body's graceful movements.

Other items used in rhythmic gymnastics move through the air differently. Compare the materials which are used to make balls, clubs, hoops, and ropes. How does the force of gravity affect them?

Each time one person climbs on top of another, the center of gravity shifts. It becomes harder and harder for the gymnasts to keep their balance.

Sports acrobatics is one of the most exciting types of gymnastics. It includes gymnasts tumbling and twisting on top of their teammates, raising partners into the air, throws, and balancing acts. Sports acrobats do not need special equipment, just floor mats. They do need strength, agility, and teamwork.

Games in the Gym

Many gyms are used for team games and sports such as basketball and volleyball. Each basketball team has five players. They pass the ball from one to another and bounce it on the ground as they run along.

The way a ball flies through the air is determined by the size and weight of the ball, the force of the throw or bounce, and the pull of gravity.

The baskets are set 10 feet above the ground, so it helps to be tall.

The ball is made of rubber, which is an elastic material. It bounces well because air inside it pushes back against the hard floor.

Volleyball can be played in a gym, too. Two teams of six players hit the ball across a net with their hands. The aim is to ground the ball so the other team cannot return it. Players must hit the ball hard and aim it well.

A volleyball is smaller than a basketball and is only half as heavy.

Words we use

acrobats: people who perform gymnastics

aerobic: using oxygen

apparatus: gymnasium equipment

artistic gymnastics: a type of gymnastics that includes vaulting, floor exercises, and exercises on the bars and beam

balance: the point at which the weight of an object or body is spread equally so that it does not topple over

balance beam: a high, narrow bar used in gymnastics

blood vessels: the small tubes that carry blood around the body

cartwheel: a gymnastic move in which the body turns upside-down onto one hand at a time and then lands on one foot at a time

circuit: a course that starts and ends in the same place

cramp: a painful tightening of the muscles

elastic: able to stretch and regain shape

evaporate: to turn from liquid into invisible gas, or vapor

flexibility: the ability to move, bend, and stretch easily

friction: the rubbing of one surface against another

gravity: the force that pulls things down towards the ground

gymnasium: a building made for physical exercise and sports

gymnasts: people who perform gymnastic exercises as a sport

handspring: a gymnastic move in which the gymnast jumps and lands on the hands, then on the feet

horizontal bar: a high bar stretched across two metal poles, used in boys' and men's gymnastics. Also called the high bar.

horse: a long padded block on legs, used for vaulting

impact: the force with which one object hits another

impetus: the force that keeps a body moving forward

lever: a bar or other rigid object that is used to make another object or body move

oxygen: a gas found in air and water that all animals need to live

parallel bars: a pair of bars set side-by-side at the same height, used in boys' and men's gymnastics

pommels: handles on a type of vaulting horse, called a pommel horse, that is used in boys' and men's gymnastics

rhythmic gymnastics: gymnasts who perform exercises in time to music, often with ribbons, hoops, and balls

roundoff: a gymnastic move similar to a cartwheel but with the landing on both feet at once

split: a gymnastic move, done in a sitting position, in which the legs are extended as far as they can go, in opposite directions

somersault: a forward or backward roll on a mat

spotter: an instructor or exercise partner who watches while you exercise to help you do the exercise correctly, without hurting yourself

streamlined: shaped to slip easily through the air

tendon: a tough cord that joins muscle to bone

thrusts: a push or force forward or upward

uneven parallel bars: a pair of bars set side-by-side with one higher than the other, used in girls' and women's gymnastics

wind resistance: the force of the air against an object moving through it

Index